**Report by the**
**Comptroller and Auditor General**

# The Millennium Threat: 221 Days and Counting

Ordered by the
House of Commons
to be printed 24 May 1999

LONDON: The Stationery Office
9.25

HC 436  Session 1998-99
Published 26 May 1999

This report has been prepared under Section 6 of the National Audit Act 1983 for presentation to the House of Commons in accordance with Section 9 of the Act.

*John Bourn*
Comptroller and Auditor General

National Audit Office
19 May 1999

The Comptroller and Auditor General is the head of the National Audit Office employing some 750 staff. He, and the National Audit Office, are totally independent of Government. He certifies the accounts of all Government departments and a wide range of other public sector bodies; and he has statutory authority to report to Parliament on the economy, efficiency and effectiveness with which departments and other bodies have used their resources.

For further information about the National Audit Office please contact:

National Audit Office
Press Office
157-197 Buckingham Palace Road
Victoria
London
SW1W 9SP

Tel: 0171-798 7400

email:nao@gtnet.gov.uk

Web site address: http://www.open.gov.uk/nao/home.htm

# Contents

# Executive summary

## What is the problem and why has it arisen?

**1**    The Year 2000 problem or "the millennium threat" has arisen because in the past computers and electronic systems have referred to years by their last two digits rather than all four ("99" rather than "1999"). As a consequence, many computer systems and other electronic equipment cannot tell the years 2000 and 1900 apart and may produce meaningless or incorrect information, or may fail completely. This Report examines how Government have reacted to safeguard essential services across the United Kingdom, and updates progress in central Government Departments and Agencies.

**2**    The millennium threat potentially affects everyone, and is not just an information technology problem. As work to counter the millennium threat has progressed, organisations have realised that it is a business wide problem affecting equipment not traditionally thought of as computers, such as telephones and security systems. In addition, organisations have had to consider how their suppliers and customers are addressing the Year 2000 problem, and plan how to maintain business continuity if any failures do arise.

**3**    For a large and complex organisation, this work could take two or three years or more, and even for a small business it could take many months.

## Who is responsible for taking action in the United Kingdom?

**4**    The millennium bug potentially affects everyone – citizens, businesses, and the public sector. Action to overcome the threat is the responsibility of individuals, individual companies, and individual public sector bodies. In the United Kingdom, the Government's approach to alerting industry to the problem and ensuring appropriate action in both the private and public sectors has evolved over the last three years.

**5**    A key development was the Prime Minister's announcement in March 1998 that the Government's overall objective was to "ensure no material disruption to the essential public services of the United Kingdom". The Government established a Ministerial Group chaired by the Lord President of the Council and Leader of the House of Commons to co-ordinate action across Government and the whole of the national infrastructure. A Year 2000 team were created in the Cabinet Office, and Action 2000, a limited company sponsored by the Government, started a programme of work to ensure "no material disruption" and sustain public confidence that essential services will continue to operate as normal over the millennium period.

**6** A wide range of public and private sector organisations deliver essential services, and most depend on each other for continuity. To promote sharing and exchange of information, Action 2000 created the National Infrastructure Forum. The Forum now comprises around 250 organisations from more than 25 sectors, private, public and regulated, who deliver essential services in the UK.

**7** For central Government, responsibility for taking action to ensure that systems are Year 2000 compliant and continuity of service rests with individual Government Departments and Agencies. Within the wider public sector, principal responsibility rests with individual bodies.

**8** Within central Government, the Cabinet Office have the lead role in monitoring progress by individual Departments and Agencies.

## What are essential services on which the public rely?

**9** To define essential services, the Cabinet Office commissioned a review to identify and map the key business processes in the UK, how they depend on each other, and the outcomes of their failure. The result was 58 high level activities (for example, "sell food to customer" - a full list is at Appendix 2) and around 1000 detailed processes.

# How can the public be confident of "no material disruption"?

**10** The next phase of the work is to assess millennium readiness of each of these processes through a UK wide programme of independent assessment to common standards and benchmarks and to publish the results. Publication provides information needed by others who are making their own business continuity plans and sustains public confidence that these essential services will continue to operate as normal over the millennium period.

**11** To ensure consistency and enable comparisons between sectors, Action 2000 have introduced a traffic light coding to indicate the status of each high level activity:

**Independent assessment programme: status indicator colour codes**

**Figure 1**

Colour code | Description

Unable to form assessment with the present level of information.

The assessment indicates that there is a severe risk of material disruption to infrastructure processes and that timely rectification may not be possible.

The assessment indicates that there is some risk of material disruption to infrastructure processes, but that there is an agreed containment plan to rectify shortcomings.

The assessment has not indicated any risks of material disruption to the infrastructure processes. (Note: green was not used because it could imply a guarantee of continuity, which cannot be given).

**12** The independent assessment programme started in October 1998 and is continuing. The work has been split into three tranches and results are generally disclosed as the assessments are completed, together with interim assessments in some sectors.

**13** The position for the first tranche was reported at the National Infrastructure Forum meeting and published on the Internet on 21 January 1999 and updated at the Forum meeting on 21 April. The position for the second tranche was also reported at the Forum meeting and published on 21 April. Independent assessment for the third tranche of sectors is now underway and disclosure is planned for July 1999.

**14** For central Government Departments and Agencies, the Cabinet Office are responsible for monitoring progress, identifying potential weaknesses and suggesting that action is taken. The Central Computer and Telecommunications Agency (CCTA), on behalf of the Cabinet Office issue questionnaires to individual Departments about every three months. These progress reviews have supported Government statements to the House of Commons roughly every three months, the most recent by Mrs Margaret Beckett, President of the Council and Leader of the House on 16 March 1999. The detailed results of these reviews are placed in the House of Commons Libraries and published on the Internet.

## What are the results on independent assessment so far?

**15** For the first tranche, the results announced on 21 April show that a good deal of progress has been made since the initial results published in January. However, a substantial amount of work remains if risks are to be fully eliminated in those areas where the current status is red (see Figure 1 for definitions) – some shippers and suppliers of gas (seven per cent), and some firms in the financial services sector (one per cent of high impact organisations, and 10 per cent of medium impact organisations).

**16** For the second tranche, the initial results on 21 April showed that most sectors were on track to achieve blue status by the end of September 1999. Again there are three areas where assessments so far reveal some red status indicators – Hospitals and Healthcare (nine per cent in England, six per cent in Wales), Fire and Rescue Services in England and Wales (two per cent), and Police in England and Wales (nine per cent), but again Action 2000 expect the position to improve.

**17** For the third tranche, assessments are currently underway, with the initial results expected from June onwards, with a formal announcement for these sectors planned for 13 July.

## Will the National Health Service be ready?

**18** Since our Report last year, the National Health Service (NHS) have made considerable progress but much remains to be done, in particular in the nine per cent of NHS bodies in England, and six per cent in Wales with a red status. The NHS also face particularly complex supply chain and resource management issues, and are planning for extra demand on their services over the millennium period, which must be reflected in business continuity plans.

## What about local government?

**19**    The Audit Commission report that in local government there is a wide variation between the best and poorest performers. The Audit Commission have asked a number of Authorities to speed up their programmes of work and, later in the year, will be reporting individually on the progress of all Local Authorities.

## How will this programme be taken forward?

**20**    Action 2000 expect the assessment and disclosure process in the national infrastructure programme to become continuous, with reassessments to cover gaps or areas where material risks remain. Action 2000 are strongly encouraging Responsible Bodies to name those organisations where there are still material risks of severe disruption later in the year.  Action 2000 also require contingency plans to be developed to ensure business continuity.

## Will central Government Departments and Agencies be ready?

**21**    Progress against the key target milestone to test, modify and re-test systems by April 1999 has slipped steadily, so that by March 1999 only 11 per cent of bodies expected to achieve it. However, Departments have prioritised work so that business critical systems have greater priority.  Although the original deadline has been missed for many business critical systems, 90 per cent of bodies expect to complete the work by the end of September 1999. But there are eight bodies where completion is expected from October to December 1999 (the Defence Evaluation and Research Agency and the Forensic Science Service in December), and there is clearly no room for further slippage. From June 1999 progress will be monitored monthly.

**22**    Only 68 per cent of bodies met the target of having initial business continuity plans in place by January 1999, and only 38 per cent included all the components necessary for a fully robust plan.

## What are the main areas of concern in the UK now?

**23**    A summary of those areas where substantial work remains if risks of material disruption are to be eliminated is set out in Figure 2.

**Areas where substantial work remains**

| Figure 2 | |
|---|---|

| Sector | Status (see Figure 1) and comments |
|---|---|
| *National infrastructure sectors* | |
| Gas – shippers and suppliers | 7% red |
| Financial Services | |
| ■ high impact organisations | 1% red |
| ■ medium impact firms | 10% red |
| Hospitals and Healthcare | |
| ■ England | 9% red |
| ■ Wales | 6% red |
| Fire and Rescue Services | 2% red |
| Police | 9% red |
| | |
| *Central Government Departments and Agencies – business critical systems* | |
| Defence Evaluation and Research Agency | Embedded systems work expected to be completed in December 1999 |
| Foreign and Commonwealth Office | IT systems work expected to be completed in October 1999, telecommunications systems in November 1999 |
| Forensic Science Service (Home Office) | Embedded systems and telecommunications systems work expected to be completed in December 1999 |
| Ministry of Defence (Centre) | IT and telecommunications systems work expected to be completed in October 1999 |
| Office for National Statistics | IT systems work expected to be completed in October 1999 |
| Procurement Executive (Ministry of Defence) | IT systems work expected to be completed in October 1999, embedded systems work in November 1999 |
| Royal Air Force | IT and embedded systems work expected to be completed in November 1999 |
| Royal Navy | IT systems work expected to be completed in October 1999 |

# What is the position overseas?

**24**　Year 2000 problems overseas could potentially cause problems in the UK, for example with the food supply chain. This aspect is covered by the national infrastructure work.

**25**　On the state of readiness in other countries, the Foreign and Commonwealth Office have issued some general advice to UK businesses with staff and offices overseas, and general advice to travellers, but this advice is not country specific. Some more country specific information is beginning to appear on the Internet.

## What emergency planning arrangements are in place?

**26** The millennium bug and millennium celebratory events add to the potential for problems or emergencies over the New Year period, and the Home Office have enhanced the existing well established emergency planning arrangements to take account of the millennium effect.

## How much will it cost?

**27** The cost of addressing the Year 2000 problem for the whole of the UK national infrastructure is not known. For Great Britain, central Government Departments and Agencies making returns estimate costs to be £420 million. The NHS in England estimate costs at approximately £321 million.

## What must happen now?

**28** Our main recommendations are that:

■ For the UK national infrastructure:

- ❑ the Cabinet Office, Action 2000, those responsible for commissioning the independent assessments, and those undertaking them should press those bodies where a material risk of disruption remains to put a robust remedial programme of work in place;

- ❑ Action 2000 and the Cabinet Office should continue the programme of independent assessment and disclosure for the key processes in the UK national infrastructure, and encourage Government Departments, Local Authorities and others providing elements of the national infrastructure to take forward the programme by focusing on emergency and continuity planning and the testing of those plans;

- ❑ Action 2000, the Cabinet Office and Responsible Bodies should keep citizens and businesses informed of where the remaining risks lie, and report progress regularly;

- ❑ the Foreign and Commonwealth Office should take action to keep citizens and businesses informed about the position in other countries.

■ For central Government Departments and Agencies, the Cabinet Office should:

❑ press those Departments where work is slipping, especially on business critical systems, to give the remaining work high priority;

❑ continue to refine the monitoring and reporting process so that priorities for attention can more easily be identified;

❑ shift attention from rectification and testing work to continuity planning and press all Departments and Agencies to put comprehensive and tested business continuity plans in place.

# Part 1: Background

## What is the problem and why has it arisen?

**1.1**   In the past computers, microprocessors and other electronic systems have referred to years by their last two digits rather than by all four (for example "99" representing 1999), to save memory space, reduce operating costs, and maintain compatibility with earlier systems. Many systems using this method of recording dates remain in operation and now cannot tell the year 2000 and the year 1900 apart as both are represented by "00". This problem is known as "the millennium threat, the millennium bug, the millennium date change, the Year 2000 problem", or simply "Year 2000" or "Y2K".

**1.2**   This means that some computers or other electronic equipment and microprocessors which use date information may produce meaningless or incorrect information, or fail completely, as the year 2000 is approached or reached.

**1.3**   The millennium threat was initially considered to be an Information Technology (IT) problem. But as testing and rectification work has progressed, many organisations have realised that it will have a much wider impact and as a result the response must be on a business wide basis – whether Government Department or Agency, or a private company. This is because:

- electronic equipment such as telephones, security systems, medical equipment and lifts, which are not traditionally thought of as computers or IT systems, may contain microprocessors which are affected by the millennium date change;

- nearly all organisations depend on others for supply of goods and services (for example, materials and utility services), and on customers. Even if an organisation's own internal systems and equipment are Year 2000 compliant, they may still be unable to continue to function if others in the supply chain fail;

- even with the best managed Year 2000 compliance programme, something may have been overlooked. All organisations need to prepare business continuity plans to deal with failures that may occur despite their preparations, and must check that their suppliers are doing likewise. As the complexity of the supply chain has become better understood, and the millennium itself draws nearer, the development of business continuity plans has become steadily more important, possibly more important than working on compliance if resources are limited.

## Lifecycle of a Year 2000 project

**1.4**    The key stages in a business wide Year 2000 project are set out in Figure 3. The timeframe for this work will vary depending on the size and complexity of the business, ranging from two or three years for a large organisation to perhaps six months for a small business.

**Lifecycle of a Year 2000 project framework**

**Figure 3**

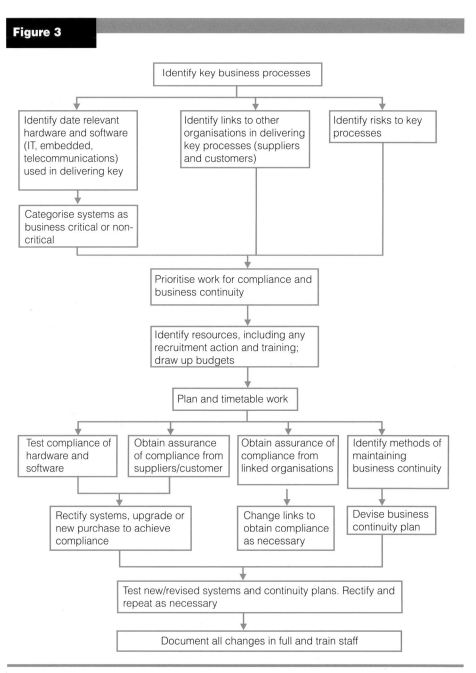

## Who is responsible for taking action to overcome the millennium threat in the United Kingdom?

**1.5**   The millennium threat potentially affects everyone – citizens, businesses in the private sector, as well as the whole of the public sector. Action to overcome the millennium threat is the responsibility of individuals, individual companies, individual Government Departments and Agencies, and other public sector bodies.

**1.6**   In the United Kingdom, the Department of Trade and Industry (DTI) initially took the lead to alert British industry to the problem and encourage them to take action to ensure millennium compliance, originally through the work of Taskforce 2000.

**1.7**   In September 1997, the Government announced the creation of Action 2000, a company limited by guarantee, and sponsored by the Department of Trade and Industry. They started work in January 1998 to work with the Government and the private sector to reduce the impact of the millennium threat on the UK economy to an acceptable risk, initially by raising business awareness and advising small and medium size enterprises.

**1.8**   In March 1998, the Prime Minister announced that the overall Government objective was to "ensure no material disruption to the essential public services of the United Kingdom" as a result of the millennium bug. The Government also established a Ministerial Group (known as "MISC4"), chaired by the President of the Council and Leader of the House of Commons, to co-ordinate action across Government Departments and the whole of the national infrastructure. At the same time, the Year 2000 Team were created in the Cabinet Office to support the Ministerial Group in driving action across the public and private sectors. They co-ordinate information and initiatives and advise Ministers on the steps that they need to take collectively to prevent damage from the Year 2000 date change.

**1.9**   From June 1998, the Cabinet Office have contributed to the funding of Action 2000, which now have four main objectives, to:

■   support the DTI by:

❑   raising awareness of the millennium bug in business;

❑   providing direct support to small and medium sized enterprises;

■  support the Cabinet Office:

❑  in reducing the risk of material disruption due to the millennium bug to essential services on which the country and individuals rely;

❑  in helping to sustain public confidence that essential services will continue to operate as normal over the millennium period.

**1.10**  Although the work of Action 2000 is focused in the United Kingdom, it also extends, to a degree, to assessing the effects of failures overseas, which could affect the UK national infrastructure.

**1.11**  A wide range of both public and private sector organisations deliver essential public services, and most services are dependent on each other for continuity, for example electricity supply requires fuel and water, and water supply requires electricity. To promote exchange of information to help meet the Government's objective, particularly because most organisations would not give a view on continuity of services without similar assurances from their suppliers, Action 2000 established a National Infrastructure Forum. The Forum currently comprises around 250 organisations from more than 25 sectors, private, public and regulated, who deliver essential services in the UK. Within the Forum, a Steering Group works on policy matters, and an Advisory Group exercises a critical review of Action 2000 activities.

**1.12**  The Cabinet Office also have the lead role in monitoring progress by central Government Departments and their Agencies through the issue of questionnaires about every three months.  The CCTA support the Cabinet Office in the development and dissemination of best practice.  The CCTA, on behalf of the Cabinet Office, issue the monitoring questionnaires to central Departments and Agencies and co-ordinate and analyse the responses.

**1.13**  Within the central Government sector, responsibility for taking action to ensure that systems are Year 2000 compliant and ensuring continuity of service remains with individual Government Departments and Agencies.

**1.14**  The relationship between these bodies is shown in Figure 4.

**Government Year 2000 framework**

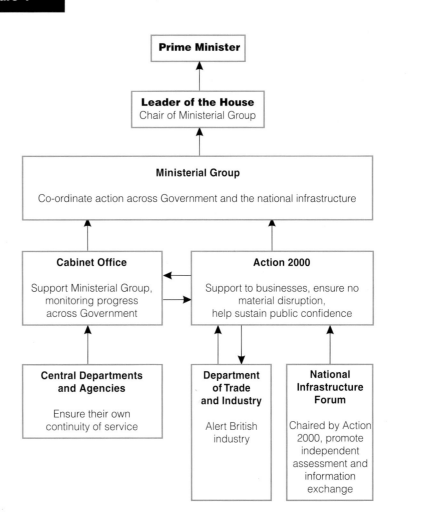

**Figure 4**

Prime Minister

Leader of the House
Chair of Ministerial Group

Ministerial Group

Co-ordinate action across Government and the national infrastructure

Cabinet Office

Support Ministerial Group, monitoring progress across Government

Action 2000

Support to businesses, ensure no material disruption, help sustain public confidence

Central Departments and Agencies

Ensure their own continuity of service

Department of Trade and Industry

Alert British industry

National Infrastructure Forum

Chaired by Action 2000, promote independent assessment and information exchange

**1.15** For the wider public sector bodies, the principal responsibility for ensuring compliance and "no material disruption" rests with those bodies.

## Earlier reports by the Comptroller and Auditor General and the Committee of Public Accounts

**1.16** This Report follows up our three earlier Reports on the Year 2000 problem:

■ "Managing the Millennium Threat" (HC 3, Session 1997-98);

■ "Managing the Millennium Threat II" (HC 724, Session 1997-98);

■ "How the Utility Regulators are addressing the Year 2000 Problem in the Utilities" (HC 222, Session 1998-99).

**1.17** The first warned about the potential consequences of the inability of computer and electronic equipment to handle the date change on 1 January 2000. The second reported on progress across the central Government sector, and described how the National Health Service and the Department of Social Security, in particular, were tackling the problem. The third examined what the utility regulators are doing to ensure that utilities are tackling the Year 2000 problem. We have also reported on specific issues and sectors as part of our wider work (for example, National Health Service Summarised Accounts in England, Scotland and Wales). Appendix 1 provides a full list of earlier reports by the Comptroller and Auditor General and Committee of Public Accounts on the Year 2000 problem.

**1.18** On the basis of our Report, "Managing the Millennium Threat II", the Committee of Public Accounts took evidence from the Office of Public Service (now the Cabinet Office) and the National Health Service Executive on progress in tackling the Year 2000 problem across central Government, the wider public sector as a whole, and within the National Health Service in England.

**1.19** In their subsequent Report ("Managing the Millennium Threat", 66th Report 1997-98 (July 1998)), the Committee recommended:

■ action by the Office of Public Service to:

    ❑ ensure that business critical systems, including those that impact directly on citizens and patients, are tackled first;

    ❑ monitor progress closely, and take or encourage direct action where progress is too slow, especially on those systems critical to public business and to public services;

    ❑ ensure that contingency plans are in place and are tested;

■ action by the National Health Service Executive to:

    ❑ take strong decisive action to ensure that all NHS organisations and GPs are fully prepared;

☐ monitor the position on medical equipment closely, and take every possible step to ensure the safety of patients;

☐ ensure that lack of resources does not result in the failure of systems and equipment that are critical to NHS services and patient care.

## Scope of this Report

**1.20** This Report looks at progress in tackling the Year 2000 threat in the key sectors of the United Kingdom (Part 2), and across central Government Departments and Agencies (Part 3).

## How have we conducted this investigation?

**1.21** Our examination has focused mainly on progress reports and surveys conducted by Action 2000, the CCTA on behalf of the Cabinet Office, the Audit Commission, and individual public sector bodies such as the National Health Service Executive.

**1.22** We plan a further progress Report in November 1999, which will also look in more detail at business continuity planning, emergency planning, and the overseas situation. Another Report in the spring of 2000 will look at what problems emerged over the millennium period and how well they were handled.

# Part 2: The UK National Infrastructure

## What are essential services in the United Kingdom?

**2.1** An early task for the Cabinet Office Year 2000 Team in their work to support the Government's objective of "no material disruption to essential public services…" was to define "essential services" and establish how they could affect each other. In some cases, this is obvious. For example, virtually all services depend on electricity. But in others, inter-dependencies are less clear and much more complicated. For example, aircraft rely on accurate weather forecasts in order to fly, and producing accurate weather forecasts relies on data from a wide variety of sources - including many overseas - telecommunications links to transmit the data, availability of computers to process it, availability of electricity to power them and so on.

**2.2** In March 1998, the Cabinet Office and Action 2000 commissioned Ernst and Young to identify (phase 1) and map (phase 2) the key processes of the United Kingdom, to show the flows, connections between them, responsibilities and outcomes of the failure of any of these processes. The results of this work were published in September 1998, and the outcome was definitions of 58 high level (for example, food distribution, welfare payment, and weather forecasting) and around 1000 detailed processes. We believe that this is the first time that such process mapping has been carried out on a national scale, and may well be unique in the world.

**2.3** A full list of the 58 high level processes is shown at Appendix 2. Figure 5 shows how delivery of an illustrative sample of these processes is spread across private companies, central Government, and the wider public sector.

**Examples of how high level activities are delivered by different sectors**

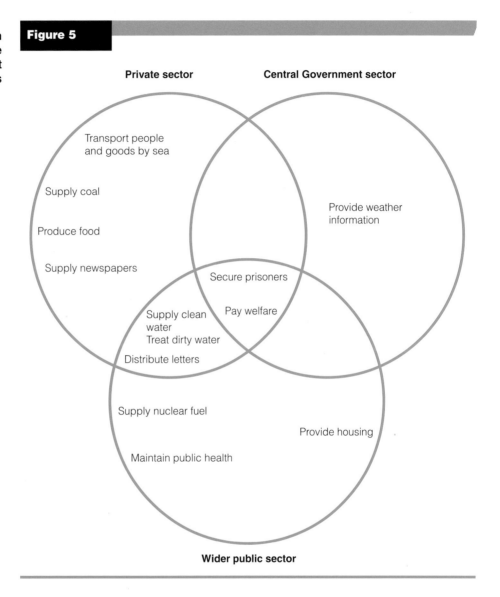

**Figure 5**

Private sector     Central Government sector

Transport people and goods by sea

Supply coal

Produce food

Supply newspapers

Provide weather information

Secure prisoners

Pay welfare

Supply clean water
Treat dirty water

Distribute letters

Supply nuclear fuel

Provide housing

Maintain public health

**Wider public sector**

## How can the public be confident of "no material disruption" for these essential services?

**2.4** The third phase of the work is to assess Year 2000 readiness for each of the services and risks to achieving "no material disruption" over the millennium period. This phase started in October 1998, and is continuing. It is being achieved through a programme of independent assessment throughout the UK (i.e. England, Wales, Scotland and Northern Ireland, but excluding Crown dependencies).

**2.5** The aim of the independent assessment programme is to ensure service suppliers' Year 2000 programmes have been properly carried out and that claims of millennium readiness are credible. Publishing the results provides reliable information that others need for their own programmes of work and continuity plans, and sustains public confidence that essential services will continue to operate.

**2.6** Action 2000, in close collaboration with the Cabinet Office:

- are co-ordinating the overall assessment programme;

- have established assessment standards and benchmarks;

- are consolidating information to assess the continuity of essential services, and publishing the overall results as the assessments are completed.

**2.7** Action 2000 have categorised the 58 high level processes identified into 25 "sectors". Each process has one or more delivery organisations. For each process, Action 2000 have identified a "Responsible Body" to:

- commission the assessment programme;

- assess the state of preparedness;

- disclose and publish the results at sector level.

**2.8** The independent assessing organisations may be industry experts, consultants, suitably qualified peer organisations, statutory auditors, statutory inspectors or regulatory bodies. A mixed approach is often the case. Details are included in Appendix 2. Both the assessing organisation and the Responsible Body can vary between England, Scotland and Wales (the position in Northern Ireland is outside the scope of this Report). To ensure that the process is independent, the service delivery body, the Responsible Body, and the assessor are normally separate bodies.

**2.9** To ensure a consistent approach and enable comparisons between sectors, Action 2000 have introduced a "traffic light" code to chart the progress of key sectors or parts of sectors towards achieving "no material disruption" over the millennium period (Figure 6).

**Independent assessment programme: status indicator colour codes**

**Figure 6**

**Colour code**    **Description**

Unable to form assessment with the present level of information.

The assessment indicates that there is a severe risk of material disruption to infrastructure processes and that timely rectification may not be possible.

The assessment indicates that there is some risk of material disruption to infrastructure processes, but that there is an agreed containment plan to rectify shortcomings.

The assessment has not indicated any risks of material disruption to the infrastructure processes. (Note: green was not used because it could imply a guarantee of continuity, which cannot be given).

**2.10** The assessment programme has been split into three tranches (Figures 7-9). Following the initial assessment and disclosure of results, gaps in the assessment and/or the need for a further assessment, and its timing, are agreed with the Responsible Body, with the results disclosed in accordance with the traffic light code. For individual processes, disclosure and publicising the results of the assessment is a function of the Responsible Body. Action 2000 are responsible for publicising the bigger picture.

## What are the results of the independent assessments so far?

**2.11** The initial results of the independent assessment of tranche 1 sectors were announced at the National Infrastructure Forum meeting on 21 January 1999, and updated at the meeting on 21 April (Figure 7). The assessments are published on the Internet by Action 2000 at **(http://www.bug2000.co.uk)** and were featured in national newspapers in mid May 1999.

# Figure 7

**Independent assessment by sector – position at 21 April 1999**

*Tranche 1*

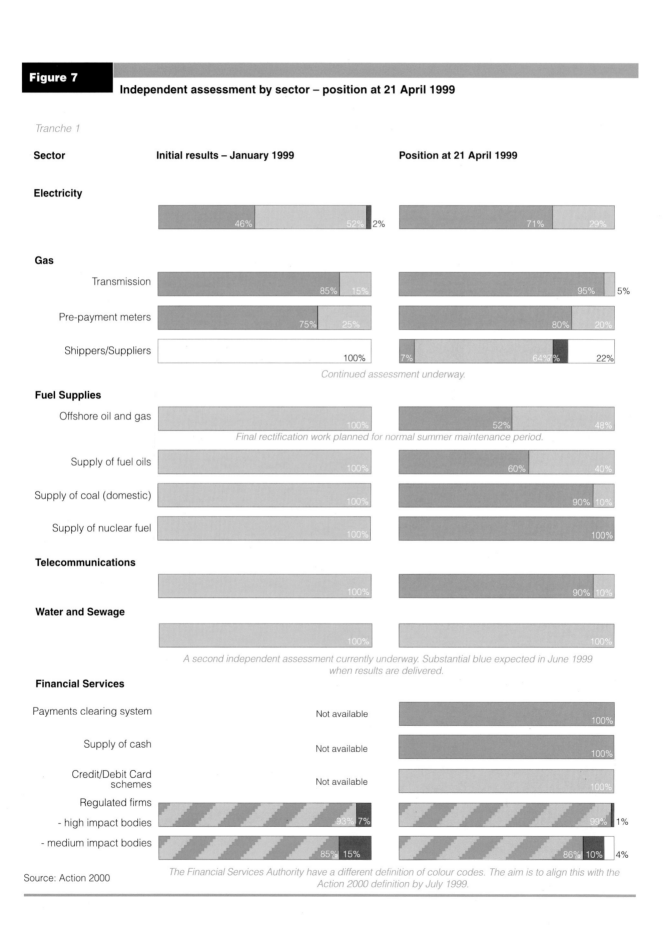

| Sector | Initial results – January 1999 | Position at 21 April 1999 |
|---|---|---|
| **Electricity** | 46% / 52% / 2% | 71% / 29% |
| **Gas** | | |
| Transmission | 85% / 15% | 95% / 5% |
| Pre-payment meters | 75% / 25% | 80% / 20% |
| Shippers/Suppliers | 100% | 7% / 64% / 7% / 22% |
| | | *Continued assessment underway.* |
| **Fuel Supplies** | | |
| Offshore oil and gas | 100% | 52% / 48% |
| | *Final rectification work planned for normal summer maintenance period.* | |
| Supply of fuel oils | 100% | 60% / 40% |
| Supply of coal (domestic) | 100% | 90% / 10% |
| Supply of nuclear fuel | 100% | 100% |
| **Telecommunications** | 100% | 90% / 10% |
| **Water and Sewage** | 100% | 100% |
| | *A second independent assessment currently underway. Substantial blue expected in June 1999 when results are delivered.* | |
| **Financial Services** | | |
| Payments clearing system | Not available | 100% |
| Supply of cash | Not available | 100% |
| Credit/Debit Card schemes | Not available | 100% |
| Regulated firms | | |
| - high impact bodies | 93% / 7% | 99% / 1% |
| - medium impact bodies | 85% / 15% | 86% / 10% / 4% |

Source: Action 2000

*The Financial Services Authority have a different definition of colour codes. The aim is to align this with the Action 2000 definition by July 1999.*

**2.12** Results of tranche 2 sectors were provided at the National Infrastructure Forum meeting on 21 April 1999. They are summarised in Figure 8. These are interim assessments based on a mixture of self and independent assessment. In most cases

---

**Figure 8**

**Interim assessment by sector – position at 21 April 1999**

*Tranche 2*

| Sector | Results |
|---|---|

**Essential Food and Groceries**

Overall — *Blue expected by end June 1999.*

Top 12 retailers

Top 20 manufacturers

Next 10 retailers

Next 50 manufacturers

**Rail Transport**

National rail overall

National rail safety systems

London underground — *Blue expected by end September 1999.*

Channel tunnel — *Blue expected by end June 1999.*

**Air Transport**

National Air Traffic Control Services — *UK processes only. Work on international dimension underway.*

UK airports and airlines — *Independent assessments are currently underway, and the results will be reported at the National Infrastructure Forum in July 1999.*

**Road Transport**

Road traffic central equipment — 98% 2%

Motorways and trunk roads England and Wales — *Blue expected by end June 1999 for England and end September 1999 for Wales.*

Scotland — 100%

Continued...

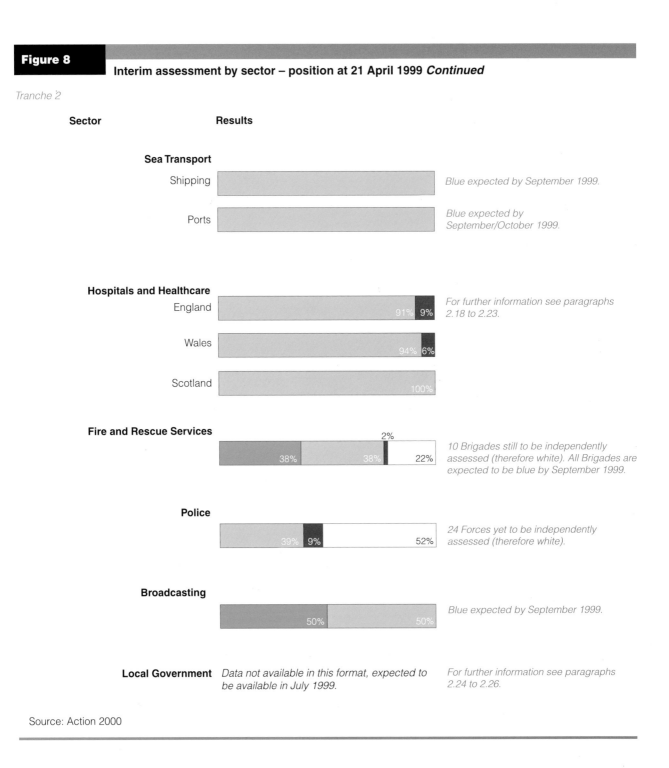

**Figure 8**

**Interim assessment by sector – position at 21 April 1999** *Continued*

*Tranche 2*

| Sector | Results | |
|---|---|---|
| **Sea Transport** | | |
| Shipping | | *Blue expected by September 1999.* |
| Ports | | *Blue expected by September/October 1999.* |
| **Hospitals and Healthcare** | | |
| England | 91% 9% | *For further information see paragraphs 2.18 to 2.23.* |
| Wales | 94% 6% | |
| Scotland | 100% | |
| **Fire and Rescue Services** | 38% 38% 2% 22% | *10 Brigades still to be independently assessed (therefore white). All Brigades are expected to be blue by September 1999.* |
| **Police** | 39% 9% 52% | *24 Forces yet to be independently assessed (therefore white).* |
| **Broadcasting** | 50% 50% | *Blue expected by September 1999.* |
| **Local Government** | *Data not available in this format, expected to be available in July 1999.* | *For further information see paragraphs 2.24 to 2.26.* |

Source: Action 2000

further work is underway. In some sectors an overall rating has been given rather than a specific percentage breakdown, which may conceal another rating for some lower level processes. Further details are on the Action 2000 Internet web site (**http://www.bug2000.co.uk**).

**2.13** The initial disclosure based mainly on the independent assessment for the tranche 3 sectors (listed in Figure 9) is planned for July 1999.

| Assessment by sector | **Figure 9** | |
| --- | --- | --- |
| | *Tranche 3* | Sea Rescue |
| | | Weather Forecasting |
| | | Post and Parcels |
| | | Welfare Payments |
| | | Flood Defence |
| | | Criminal Justice |
| | | Tax Collection |
| | | Bus Transport |
| Source: Action 2000 | | Newspaper Publishing and Distribution |

**2.14** An example of how this assessment process has been tackled and reported - in part of one sector – is shown in Figure 10.

## National Health Service and Local Authorities in England

**2.15** Two key sectors within tranche two are Hospitals and Healthcare and Local Government. Following our previous Report ("Managing the Millennium Threat II"), the Committee of Public Accounts expressed concerns about progress towards millennium readiness in the National Health Service (see paragraph 1.19).

**2.16** The Audit Commission have also produced two reports, "A Stitch in Time" (June 1998) and an update, "Time Marches On" (November 1998) which report on action being taken by local government, the NHS and the emergency services to tackle the risks associated with the Year 2000. A further update is planned for the summer of 1999.

**2.17** Progress in these two sectors is summarised in paragraphs 2.18 to 2.26.

## Figure 10

### Case Study: Independent assessment in the rail transport sector

**Rail Transport**

This case study looks at two closely related high level processes: transportation of people and goods by rail; and provision of rail infrastructure. It sets out who is responsible for ensuring continuity over the millennium period, how the assessment process has worked both within the industry and independently, and the results of the assessments.

**Who is responsible?**

This case study covers mainstream rail transport only. Even though services are provided by a number of train operating companies, the national industry network remains highly integrated and many systems interlink. There are also critical dependencies on suppliers. Similar work to identify "Responsible Bodies" and undertake independent assessment of millennium preparedness has been undertaken in other rail transport areas - London Underground, other light railways and Eurotunnel as part of tranche 2 of the Action 2000 assessment project. Other light railways will be assessed as part of tranche 3. For mainstream rail transport, responsibilities are set out in the boxes below:

| Co-ordination of Activity | Safety | Business Continuity | Responsible Bodies | Independent Assessment |
|---|---|---|---|---|
| Rail Millennium Programme Office | Railtrack<br><br>Train Operating Companies | Train Operating Companies<br><br>Railtrack | Her Majesty's Railways Inspectorate (safety)<br><br>Office of the Rail Regulator (business continuity) | W S Atkins (Year 2000 action and business continuity under the direction of the Office of the Rail Regulator)<br><br>HMRI (safety) |

**Co-ordination of activity**

Despite privatisation, the industry's response to the Year 2000 problem has been strongly co-ordinated, with Railtrack serving as controller for the national rail infrastructure and instrumental in setting up the Rail Millennium Programme Office, a cross industry body, towards the end of 1997. The Office produced a cross-industry plan, which initially focussed strongly on assessment and remediation then latterly on business continuity. Safety is the concern of all industry parties but Railtrack, due to their position as infrastructure controller, and in approving safety cases of operators on their network, play the major part.

**Safety**

*Initial work by the industry*

Railtrack introduced a dedicated Unit to review compliance issues at the beginning of 1997. The Unit set up procedures for assessing the compliance of information systems, related infrastructure (e.g. embedded systems) and suppliers. In the specific area of safety, an HMRI assessment at the end of 1998 rated its status as blue - no risks of material disruption.

*Independent assessment and the position now*

Railtrack's documentation of their work and reviews allowed the "Responsible Body" - Her Majesty's Railway Inspectorate, part of the Health and Safety Executive - to monitor the work of Railtrack and the Rail Millennium Programme Office. This monitoring covered work on inventory compilation, compliance assessment and management systems, and measured progress against the railways' own work plans. The work confirmed the Inspectorate's view that they had been right to accept Railtrack's view of the position and the rating for primary safety areas remains at blue.

Continued.

**Figure 10**

**Case Study: Rail Transport** *continued*

**Business continuity**

*Initial work by the industry*

The industry started work in early 1998 and a self-assessment at the end of that year concluded that the overall rating was amber - some risks of material disruption, but plans to rectify shortcomings were in place.

*Independent assessment and the position now*

In August 1998, the Office of the Rail Regulator issued a structured and comprehensive self-assessment questionnaire and the results largely supported the amber rating. To provide a more detailed assessment and independent view, and to ensure that supply chain issues had been addressed and that business continuity plans were comprehensive and robust, the Office of the Rail Regulator appointed independent consultants in February 1999 to examine the industry's compliance status, including compliance of key suppliers. Their work is continuing, but on the basis of results so far, an assessment as amber was announced on 21 April. The continued amber rating is primarily due to the existence of key shared systems that are operated across the industry and which are dependent on third party suppliers. In this area, better documentary evidence of compliance is needed to ensure that parties to the supply arrangements have completed their role in assessment and remediation of compliance issues as best as possible. The independent assessment has also confirmed that whilst work is still outstanding this is at the moment proceeding to planned timescales.

# Progress in the National Health Service

**2.18** The National Health Service Executive are undertaking close monitoring of progress across the Service and are the Responsible Body under the national infrastructure programme. We have examined reports by Regional Office Directors to the National Health Service Executive covering the position as at 31 December 1998.

**2.19** Of the 505 NHS organisations monitored, 460 fell into progress bands of satisfactory or making good progress. This left 45 (nine per cent) in the third band of unsatisfactory or requiring significant action in many areas to bring the project back on schedule. This was a slight improvement on the previous quarter's position.

**2.20** Figure 11 shows the position by type of body, which was also reported to the National Infrastructure Forum on 21 April 1999:

**Progress in NHS England by type of body - position at 21 April 1999**

**Figure 11**

| Type of body | Results |
|---|---|
| All NHS organisations | 91% 9% |
| Acute, Combined and Community Trusts | 92% 8% |
| Ambulance Trusts | 86% 14% |
| Health Authorities | 88% 12% |

Source: NHS Executive

## Costs

**2.21** The cost of Year 2000 work in all NHS Trusts and Health Authorities in England was reported to be £321 million.

## What are the main issues affecting the National Health Service?

**2.22** Returns from the eight National Health Service regions in England raised a number of key issues of concern if "no material disruption" is to be achieved over the millennium period:

- **Supply chain** - Managing the supply chain has emerged as one of the most difficult and complex compliance strands to manage across the NHS. The most common problems reported include identifying all suppliers and obtaining reliable and meaningful product and service compliance statements from them. The NHS Executive have put in place a number of central schemes to secure the supply of essential products, such as drugs, throughout the millennium period and beyond. This includes a pharmaceutical alliance to secure supply and availability of drugs, and a supply chain assurance scheme for commodities and medical products.

- **Human resources** - The NHS are particularly dependent on their staff to ensure continuity of service over the millennium period. Continuity planners report difficulty in estimating the impacts of staff absenteeism, seasonal illnesses and the extra demands for services made by the general public. The

Government decided against any new specific national pay agreement or additional funding for extra payments to staff, but central guidance has been issued, explaining that local staffing arrangements, in consultation with local staff representatives, should be made.

- **Conflicting and competing priorities** - The emphasis of Year 2000 work is, quite rightly, moving from system testing and fixing to plan for business continuity, contingency and emergency. Several health organisations have reported difficulties in drawing up necessary plans because of the conflicting and competing priorities, including:

  - lack of consistency between health organisations and regions over the priority of each of the main tasks;

  - competition for resources with longer running projects, such as waiting list targets and the organisationís own Information Strategy;

  - change in project management responsibilities because of Trust and Health Authority mergers.

## Action taken

**2.23** The NHS Executive have issued guidance and taken action to help resolve these issues. The Executive are focusing on those areas where there is severe risk of material disruption (colour code red) and plan to publish the results of further progress reviews and independent assessments, as they become available, with a further public statement in July.

## Progress in Local Authorities in England

**2.24** The Audit Commission are monitoring progress in local government in England and Wales. The Commission's work in this area is also being used as the form of independent assessment for local government for the national infrastructure programme. The Commission's approach to date has been to compare data from a rolling programme of independent reviews carried out in the six monthly periods. The data summarised below compares performance in the six months to March 1999 with reviews undertaken in the six months to March 1998, and September 1998 to provide a view of progress. This is also compared against a best practice benchmark which shows where Year 2000 projects should be at any point in time. Summary monitoring information is provided to the Cabinet Office, Responsible Bodies and published on the Internet.

**2.25** The Audit Commission report that, on average, progress has been significant in all types of authority, but remains behind the best practice benchmark, and much remains to be done. There is also a wide variation between the best and the poorest performers. The Audit Commission are monitoring progress under seven headings, and the latest returns are summarised below:

- **Awareness** - Senior management are well briefed, 90 per cent of Authorities are regularly bringing Year 2000 issues to their staff's attention and have mechanisms in place to capture information about Year 2000 problems.

- **Project formation** - Almost all Authorities have established multi-disciplinary project teams, over 75 per cent have established a specific Year 2000 budget, and 90 per cent have estimated the staffing resources required.

- **Scoping** - 95 per cent of Authorities have completed or are close to completing an inventory of equipment and contracts, with the remaining areas of doubt relating to inventories of embedded systems. 90 per cent have contacted key suppliers and two-thirds are pursuing ambiguous or nil responses.

- **Prioritisation** – Over 80 per cent of Authorities have determined which systems, equipment or services must take priority.

- **Procurement** - Almost all Authorities have amended purchasing guidelines and equipment specifications to ensure that new purchases are Year 2000 compliant, and half have reviewed their existing support and maintenance contracts.

- **Testing** – Two-thirds of Authorities have developed strategies for testing equipment, systems, and external services. However, many smaller councils do not have the resources to undertake large scale testing of major systems and are relying on suppliers' assurances and delivery of compliant software.

- **Continuity planning** – Three-quarters of Authorities have started continuity planning, but lack of information about the continuity of utility supplies (but which is now available through the work of Action 2000 and the National Infrastructure Forum) was reported to be making the process more difficult. The availability of staff with the right skills at the right time is a major issue for all Authorities. Emergency planning units are actively involved with Year 2000 work in 92 per cent of authorities.

**2.26** The Audit Commission have asked some Authorities to speed up Year 2000 work and, later in the year, plan to report individually on the position of all Authorities.

## Further action

**2.27** For all 58 activities key to continuity of normal business in the UK, Action 2000 expect the independent assessment and reporting process to become continuous, with the results of work to cover gaps and further assessments published as they are completed. They plan to take this process forward later in the year by encouraging Responsible Bodies to name those organisations where there is still a severe risk of material disruption (colour code, red), where this is legally possible. This procedure will cascade information from a national picture to a more local level so that citizens and businesses will be able to more easily assess how they might be affected.

**2.28** Action 2000 also plan to focus the work of the National Infrastructure Forum on business continuity planning, and the testing of those plans, as the year progresses.

## Emergency planning in the United Kingdom

**2.29** Both the millennium bug and millennium celebratory events add to the potential for problems or emergencies over the New Year period.

**2.30** To counter potential problems arising over the millennium period, the Home Office have devoted effort, in conjunction with Local Authorities, the emergency services, the utility companies and Government Departments to make sure that the systems that help them deal with emergencies are themselves Year 2000 compliant. This work includes an element of independent assessment.

**2.31** There are comprehensive and well developed arrangements for dealing with emergencies in the United Kingdom. Clear roles have been established for Local Authorities, the emergency services and key utilities. If necessary, mutual support can be offered and additional help may be available from the military. For major disasters, depending on the scale and nature, specific Government Departments may step in and take the lead.

**2.32** The various arrangements are described in detail in the Home Office booklet "Dealing with Disaster", which sets out Government policies in this area.

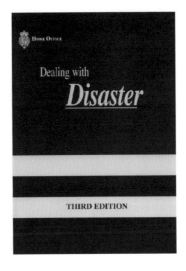

**2.33** Despite best efforts, unforeseen disaster could nevertheless arise. Local Authorities may also find that the normal mutual arrangements cannot be relied upon, and that any help from the military will be severely limited by other pressures. Effort has therefore been devoted into enhancing the normal arrangements. For example, additional millennium events have been held at the Emergency Planning College, Local Authorities have incorporated Year 2000 elements into their exercise programmes, and the emergency services have been working with Action 2000 and the National Infrastructure Forum. A series of joint regional events have already been held, and more are planned, involving the Emergency Planning College, the Emergency Planning Society, and the Local Government Association.

## The overseas position

**2.34** Year 2000 problems in overseas countries could potentially lead to difficulties in the UK, for example, with food supply. Action 2000 have formed an International Sub-Group, of the Foreign and Commonwealth Office and others, which is addressing this issue as part of the national infrastructure work.

**2.35** Outside the infrastructure work, the Foreign and Commonwealth Office have advised UK businesses that they need to consider how Year 2000 problems overseas could impact on their operations and have suggested issues that companies should explore with their overseas partners, suppliers and customers. Where UK companies have overseas offices, or staff abroad, the Foreign and Commonwealth Office have suggested that they assess local risks to continuity of operations and health and safety of staff, although obtaining reliable information in some locations may not be easy.

**2.36** The Foreign and Commonwealth Office have also issued general advice to travellers overseas which warns of potential disruption caused by the millennium threat and advises them to seek advice from travel agents and airlines on how potential problems are being addressed at their planned destination. United Kingdom diplomatic and consular posts are preparing to provide the usual range of assistance and protection over the millennium change-over period, although local disruption to essential services may temporarily affect the level of this service.

**2.37** However, the Foreign and Commonwealth Office have not yet provided country specific advice because of the difficulty in obtaining verifiable data. They are working with other Government Departments, international organisations and multinational forums to try to improve the quality of information available to build up a picture of global readiness to ensure that the interests of industry and the public are protected.

**2.38** Advice on the position in specific countries is beginning to appear on the Internet. For example, the Department of State in the United States have provided a report on global readiness for the Special Committee on the Year 2000 Technology Problem for the United States Senate, which has been published on the Internet **(http://www.state.gov/www/dept/oig/library/html)** (although this is not an official United States Government report). This gives some information on sectors in groups of countries (industrialised, developing, eastern bloc), and some examples of specific countries where information has previously been discussed in the press or other public venues.

**2.39** In January 1999, the World Bank reported on the Internet **(http://worldbank.org/extdr/extme/2078.htm)** that in a Bank survey of Year 2000 preparedness in 139 developing countries, only 54 had initiated national Year 2000 policies and just 21 were taking concrete remedial steps to safeguard their computing systems. 33 countries reported high to medium awareness of the problem but were not currently taking any action. The Bank also warned that the mere existence of a Year 2000 national action plan should not be taken to imply that countries would be fully compliant by the end of 1999.

# Conclusions

## Will essential services be disrupted over the millennium period?

**2.40** Overall, the Action 2000 programme of work to identify key processes in the UK national infrastructure, map dependencies, and assess progress towards "no material disruption" has resulted in a systematic and rigorous review of compliance work and continuity planning across essential service providers over both public and private sectors.

**2.41** Those sectors in tranche 1 have made much progress since January as the independent assessment programme has continued, with a large number of amber ratings moving to blue (see Figure 6 for full definitions). However, a substantial amount of work remains to be done if risks are to be fully eliminated in those areas where the current status is red - some gas shippers and suppliers (seven per cent), and some firms in the financial services sector (one per cent of high impact bodies, and 10 per cent for medium impact bodies).

**2.42** For tranche 2 sectors, the initial results of the assessment programme reveal mostly "no risk of material disruption" ratings (blue) and "some risk of material disruption, but plan to rectify shortcomings in place" (amber) ratings. Action 2000 expect the sectors to be mostly rated blue by the end of September, but there are currently three sectors with some "severe risk of material disruption" (red) status indictors – Hospitals and Healthcare (nine per cent in England and six per cent in Wales), Fire and Rescue Services in England and Wales (two per cent) and Police in England and Wales (nine per cent).

**2.43** For sectors in the third tranche, the initial results of the independent assessment programme will be announced in July. Overall, a substantial amount of work remains to be done if risks of material disruption are to be fully eliminated.

### Will there be disruption overseas?

**2.44** Many overseas countries are not as well prepared as the UK for Year 2000 and some countries may have problems. The Foreign and Commonwealth Office are trying to build a picture of global readiness and improve the quality of information available, but have yet to issue specific country advice.

## Recommendations

**2.45** In the light of these findings we recommend that:

- the Cabinet Office, Action 2000, Responsible Bodies and independent assessors should press those bodies where there is a risk of material disruption over the millennium period to put a robust programme of remedial work in place;

- Action 2000 and the Cabinet Office continue the programme of independent assessment with Responsible Bodies and their work to sustain public confidence in "no material disruption" through disclosure and publicising the results;

- Action 2000 and the Cabinet Office should encourage Government Departments, Local Authorities and others providing elements of the national infrastructure to take forward the programme by focusing on emergency planning, continuity planning and testing of those plans;

- Action 2000, the Cabinet Office and Responsible Bodies keep citizens and businesses informed of where the remaining risks lie, and report progress regularly;

- the Foreign and Commonwealth Office take action to keep citizens and businesses informed about the position overseas.

# Part 3: Progress by Central Government

## Who is responsible for taking action to overcome the millennium threat in central Government Departments and Agencies?

**3.1** For central Government Departments and Agencies, Departments are responsible for their own compliance programme. Individual Departments also lead on areas of the wider public sector and the private sector for which they have sponsoring interests.

**3.2** Where we audit a body, we have sought a specific acknowledgement of accounting officer responsibilities for Year 2000 issues as part of the letter of representation to support their financial statements to ensure that Year 2000 issues are receiving proper attention at the highest level within all audited bodies.

## Who is responsible for monitoring progress?

**3.3** As described in Part 1, the Cabinet Office (earlier the Office of Public Service) have an overview role to monitor and publicise progress, identify potential weaknesses, suggest action, and provide guidance. They have been monitoring progress by some individual Departments and their Agencies through the issue of questionnaires about every three months. The frequency will increase to monthly from June 1999.

**3.4** From June 1998 these reviews were expanded to include selected bodies in the wider public sector, which provide elements of the public infrastructure. This area has now largely been subsumed in the national infrastructure work.

**3.5** The progress reviews have supported Government statements to the House of Commons: the first in March 1998, then June, September and November, with the most recent by Mrs Margaret Beckett, President of the Council and Leader of the House of Commons, on 16 March 1999. The data supporting these statements were collected a little earlier; for example the bulk of the data supporting the most recent statement were collected at around the end of January 1999 and progress reported to the House in March 1999 was a forecast of the position at that time.

**3.6** The results of the surveys, together with the Departments' and Agencies' original plans and other additional information, have been placed in the House of Commons Libraries and published on the Internet at **(http//www.open.gov.uk/citu/y2000.htm).**

**3.7** These arrangements cover Scotland and Wales, with the Scottish Office and the Welsh Office providing returns. With the agreement of the Northern Ireland Office, the arrangements also cover Government Departments in Northern Ireland. The summarised results are also published on the Internet at the address in paragraph 3.6, although progress in Northern Ireland is outside the scope of our Report.

## Coverage of returns

**3.8** The number of returns has grown steadily. There were 81 returns for the March 1999 review. A full list is at Appendix 3. The level of detail varies, with some Departments submitting detailed returns for quite small bodies and others providing a comprehensive but less detailed return covering all bodies.

## Progress in meeting target dates

**3.9** It was the Government's initial intention that all Departments should have:

- completed an audit of their information systems by January 1997;

- prepared a prioritised, costed and timed programme of action by October 1997;

- tested modified systems by January 1999 (or April 1999 for financial systems).

**3.10** From all Departments and Agencies initially expecting to meet these dates, overall progress has slipped steadily. For example, for business critical IT systems, the percentage of bodies expecting to complete work by the target date had fallen from 100 per cent to 86 per cent by June 1998, and 37 per cent by March 1999.

**3.11** In the following paragraphs we highlight the conclusions drawn from our examination of the quarterly returns, in terms of:

- ❏ business critical IT systems (paragraph 3.12);

- ❏ business critical embedded systems (paragraph 3.13);

- ❏ business critical telecommunications systems (paragraph 3.14);

- ❏ non-critical systems (paragraphs 3.16 to 3.17);

- ❏ availability of skills and resources (paragraphs 3.18 to 3.20);

- ❏ compliance of the supply chain (paragraphs 3.21 to 3.23);

- ❏ creating tested business continuity plans (paragraphs 3.24 to 3.25);

- ❏ overall cost estimates (paragraph 3.26);

- ❏ independent validation of plans (paragraph 3.27).

# Progress on business critical IT systems

**3.12** For business critical IT systems:

- between June 1998 and March 1999, the number of bodies who are millennium compliant has increased from two to 17 (of 77);

- in June 1998, only 10 bodies expected work to be completed after March 1999. By the March 1999 return, 47 bodies did not expect to achieve compliance by April, and six expected this work to be completed in October 1999 or later. Although the majority of bodies expect to complete work by the end of September 1999, the Ministry of Defence (MOD) expect to complete final work in December 1999 (Figures 12 and 15).

**How estimated completion dates have slipped for business critical IT systems**

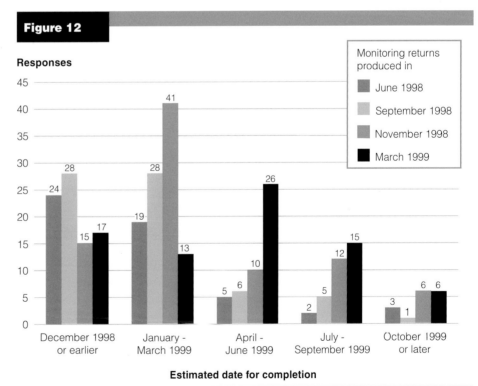

**Figure 12**

**Responses**

Monitoring returns produced in
- June 1998
- September 1998
- November 1998
- March 1999

**Estimated date for completion**

Source: Central Departments' and Agencies' monitoring returns

## Progress on business critical embedded systems

**3.13** On business critical embedded systems:

- between June 1998 and March 1999 the number of bodies who are millennium compliant has increased from five to 18 (of 79);

- for four bodies work is expected to be completed in October 1999 or later, including the Forensic Science Service and the Defence Evaluation and Research Agency in December 1999 (Figures 13 and 15).

**How estimated completion dates have slipped for business critical embedded systems**

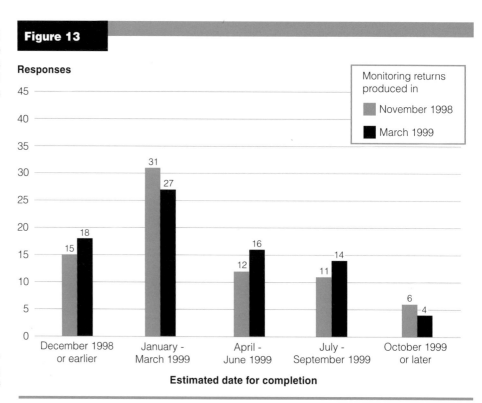

Figure 13

Source: Central Departments' and Agencies' monitoring returns

# Progress on business critical telecommunications systems

**3.14** On business critical telecommunications systems:

■ between June 1998 and March 1999 the number of bodies who are millennium compliant has increased from five to 21 (of 80);

■ three bodies expect to complete work in October 1999 or later, including the Forensic Science Service in December 1999 (Figures 14 and 15);

■ analysis of expected times to complete from successive returns suggests that time is being steadily lost, and programmes must be adequately resourced to ensure compliance is achieved.

**How estimated completion dates have slipped for business critical telecommunications systems**

**Figure 14**

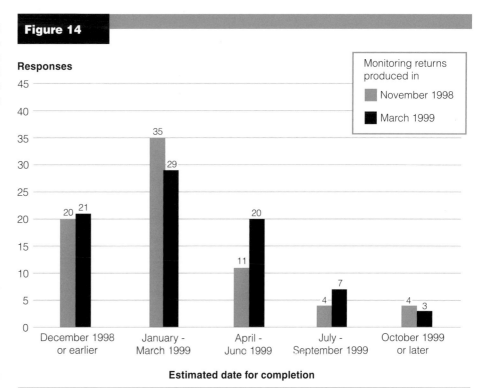

Source: Central Departments' and Agencies' monitoring returns

**3.15** Figure 15 lists, for all business critical systems, those bodies with expected completion dates of October 1999, or later.

**Business critical systems: bodies with estimated completion dates from October to December 1999**

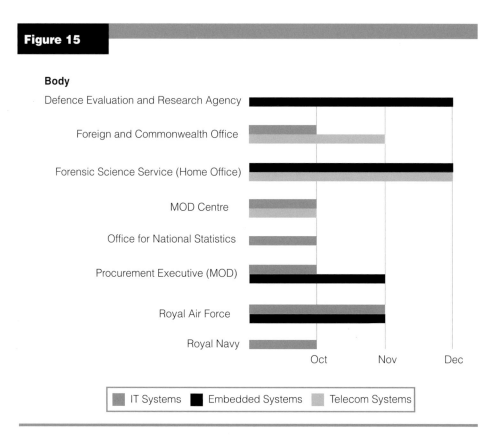

**Figure 15**

Body

Defence Evaluation and Research Agency

Foreign and Commonwealth Office

Forensic Science Service (Home Office)

MOD Centre

Office for National Statistics

Procurement Executive (MOD)

Royal Air Force

Royal Navy

Oct　Nov　Dec

■ IT Systems　■ Embedded Systems　■ Telecom Systems

Source: Central Departments' and Agencies' monitoring returns

## Progress on non-critical systems

**3.16** By definition, non-critical systems have lower priority in a millennium compliance programme. But their failure may still cause inconvenience and additional work. Successive monitoring returns report significant slippage in this area.

**3.17** Non-critical systems have again been categorised into IT, embedded systems and telecommunications systems:

■ **Non-critical IT systems:** the latest review shows that 10 bodies are now reporting compliance dates of October 1999 or later, including most parts of the Ministry of Defence (December 1999), the Home Office (centre) (January 2000) and the Foreign and Commonwealth Office and the Office of National Statistics (both March 2000);

■ **Non-critical embedded systems:** seven bodies do not expect to be compliant before October 1999, including the HM Customs and Excise and the Home Office (centre) (both December 1999), and the Defence Evaluation and Research Agency (March 2000);

■ **Non-critical telecommunications systems:** four bodies do not expect to achieve compliance before October 1999, including the Defence Evaluation and Research Agency (March 2000).

## Availability of skills and resources

**3.18** Over the past two years, many commentators have warned that the fixed deadline for achieving millennium compliance would increase competition for skills and resources and drive up salaries and prices, and forecast that in some cases staff resources necessary would not be available. This aspect has been monitored since February 1998.

**3.19** At that time, nine of 57 respondents (16 per cent) foresaw difficulties in having sufficient staff resources available to carry through the planned work and 12 were taking special steps such as prioritising work and obtaining outside assistance. Although the position worsened during 1998, by March 1999 only seven per cent of bodies were reporting insufficient resources (Figure 16).

**Availability of resources**  **Figure 16**

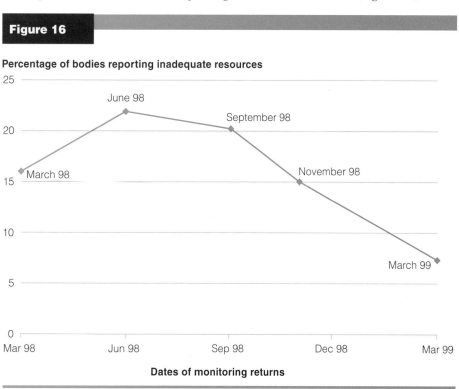

**Percentage of bodies reporting inadequate resources**

Source: Central Departments' and Agencies' monitoring returns

**Dates of monitoring returns**

**3.20** Resource difficulties are reported to have been overcome by conducting special recruiting exercises and by implementing improved pay packages in order to help retain the relevant staff. About 40 per cent of bodies reported such actions in the November 1998 review. In addition, bodies have diverted resources from other work, often by postponing enhancements or minor development work. 32 per cent of respondents reported this action in November 1998, with five bodies having postponed major developments and two had stopped all other work. By March 1999, a further nine bodies had begun diverting resources, with three others delaying work on additional major systems.

## Compliance of supply chain

**3.21** Departments and Agencies are both ensuring that:

- system components (e.g. hardware and software) supplied from outside are millennium compliant;

- providers of core outsourced services and more general outside supplies are themselves millennium compliant, and will continue to function over the century date change.

**3.22** On average, bodies report that satisfactory assurances have been received for 75 per cent of business links, whether customers or suppliers. For information technology component suppliers, between March 1998 and March 1999 steady progress has been made and latest returns show that 90 per cent of the links identified have received satisfactory assurances from suppliers (Figure 17).

**3.23** Although only 31 per cent of bodies were satisfied that all their links were millennium resistant, i.e. that they were to bodies who would themselves continue functioning, the great majority of the others were satisfied with most of their links.

## Business continuity planning

**3.24** In response to the Report from the Committee of Public Accounts (66th Report, 1997-98), the Cabinet Office asked all Departments and Agencies to develop initial business continuity plans by January 1999 and update them as their programmes of work mature and risks become clearer as the year progresses. They have also specified key components of plans, including assessment of risk, inclusion of key milestones for completion of plans, identification of required resources, and consideration of measures to ease pressure on the business process, to ensure that plans are comprehensive and robust.

**Progress on satisfactory assurances from IT component suppliers**

**Figure 17**

**Percentage reporting satisfactory assurance**

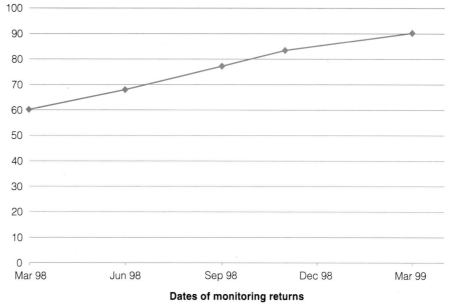

Source: Central Departments' and Agencies' monitoring returns

**Dates of monitoring returns**

**3.25** In the March 1999 review, 68 per cent of respondents had initial plans by the January 1999 target date (Figure 18), with a further 20 per cent expecting to have them in place by the end of March. However, only 38 per cent of respondents had all key components included.

**Progress in developing business continuity plans: position at January 1999 target date**

**Figure 18**

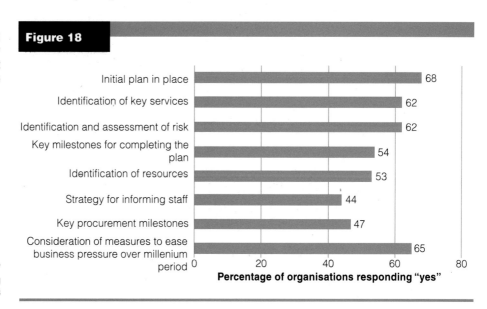

| | |
|---|---|
| Initial plan in place | 68 |
| Identification of key services | 62 |
| Identification and assessment of risk | 62 |
| Key milestones for completing the plan | 54 |
| Identification of resources | 53 |
| Strategy for informing staff | 44 |
| Key procurement milestones | 47 |
| Consideration of measures to ease business pressure over millenium period | 65 |

**Percentage of organisations responding "yes"**

Source: Central Departments' and Agencies' monitoring returns

# Overall cost estimates

**3.26** In our Report, "Managing the Millennium Threat II" (HC 724, Session 1997-98), we stated that in March 1998 Departments and Agencies estimated the cost of millennium compliance work as £393 million. In March 1999, the overall estimate has risen to £420 million (excluding the National Health Service), with the nine largest returns accounting for 85 per cent of the total costs.

# Independent validation

**3.27** The Cabinet Office have collected information about independent validation of plans and rectification work. Overall 81 per cent of bodies have had a review carried out independently of those undertaking the work. The latest returns show 58 per cent of bodies having an external assessment and 67 per cent having an internal one (for example by internal auditors). Of the assessments completed, 96 per cent looked at the management process, but only 35 per cent validated a sample of rectification work.

# Conclusions

### Will central Government Departments and Agencies be ready in time?

**3.28** Much progress has been made overall, although there is considerable slippage against completing the work by the original target dates of January and April 1999. The differentiation between business critical and non-critical systems has helped prioritise Year 2000 work. The majority of Departments and Agencies now expect to complete their work on business critical systems by the end of September 1999, but for the eight bodies with completion dates of October 1999 or later there is clearly no room for further slippage.

### Do Departments and Agencies have the necessary skilled staff?

**3.29** Overall, Departments and Agencies have suffered some shortages, but they have taken action to overcome them, including paying higher salaries and diverting staff from other projects. So the overall effect has been to defer or slow down work in other areas.

### Are business continuity plans in place?

**3.30** Continuity planning has also made progress generally and risks of failure are being addressed. But by the Cabinet Office target date, 32 per cent of bodies did not have initial plans in place and 62 per cent of bodies must widen the scope of their plans if they are to be comprehensive and robust.

### What will it cost?

**3.31** Cost estimates reported for central Departments and Agencies have increased by seven per cent since our Report "Managing the Millennium Threat II", but appear to have stabilised at around £420 million.

### Is progress being monitored satisfactorily?

**3.32** Since our Report "Managing the Millennium Threat II", the Cabinet Office have expanded coverage of monitoring returns, and redesigned them to enable easier comparisons between replies and quicker identification of changes in progress. This has enabled the Cabinet Office to more easily identify Departments and Agencies where progress is slipping, and most at risk of failure, and determine priorities for further action. Monitoring returns are reported to Parliament, placed in the Libraries of the House of Commons and published on the Internet.

## Recommendations

**3.33** In the light of these findings we recommend that the Cabinet Office should:

- press those Departments and Agencies where work is slipping, especially on business critical systems (Figure 15) to give the remaining work high priority;

- continue to refine the monitoring process so that priorities for attention can be more easily identified;

- shift attention from rectification and testing work to continuity planning, and press all Departments and Agencies to put comprehensive and tested continuity plans in place.

# Appendix 1
# Reports by the Comptroller and Auditor General and the Committee of Public Accounts

## Comptroller and Auditor General

Managing the Millennium Threat ................................................................HC 3, 1997-98

Financial Auditing and Reporting: 1996-97
General Report of the Comptroller and Auditor General................HC 251-XIX, 1997-98

National Health Service (Scotland)
Summarised Accounts 1996-97 ........................................................HC 692, 1997-98

Managing the Millennium Threat II.............................................................HC 724, 1997-98

Appropriation Accounts 1997-98 Volume 16:
Departments of the Chancellor of the Exchequer ...............................HC 1-XIV, 1997-98

How the Utility Regulators are addressing the Year 2000
Problem in the Utilities.........................................................................HC 222, 1998-99

National Health Service (Wales)
Summarised Accounts 1997-98 ........................................................HC 261, 1998-99

Financial Auditing and Reporting: 1997-98
General Report of the Comptroller and Auditor General ....................HC 1-XIX, 1998-99

National Health Service (England)
Summarised Accounts 1997-98.........................................................HC 382, 1998-99

## Committee of Public Accounts

Managing the Millennium Threat (66th Report 1997-98) ............................HC 816, 1997-98

National Health Service (Scotland)
Summarised Accounts 1996-97 (2nd Report 1998-99) ......................HC 102, 1998-99

# Appendix 2
# High level processes

A3 Fold out overleaf

| | Independent Assessor(s) |
|---|---|
| gulation | Merz & McClellan |
| | WS Atkins |
| nd Industry | WS Atkins |
| nd Industry | Aon Risk Services |
| spectorate | Nuclear Installations Inspectorate |
| nd Industry | WS Atkins |
| cations | WS Atkins |
| es, Scottish Office | Montgomery Watson; Halcrow |
| es, Scottish Office | Montgomery Watson; Halcrow |
| hority, Bank of England | Financial Services Authority/Bank of England |
| hority, Bank of England | Financial Services Authority |
| hority, Bank of England | Financial Services Authority |
| hority, Bank of England | Financial Services Authority |
| roceries Steering Group | To be appointed |
| roceries Steering Group | To be appointed |
| roceries Steering Group | To be appointed |
| roceries Steering Group | To be appointed |
| roceries Steering Group | To be appointed |
| lator, Her Majesty's Rail Inspectorate | WS Atkins |
| lator, Her Majesty's Rail Inspectorate | WS Atkins |
| London, Scottish Office | Audit Commission |
| mmission | Safety Authority |
| mmission | Safety Authority |
| | Atomic Energy Authority Technologies Limited |
| | Atomic Energy Authority Technologies Limited |
| ment, Transport and Regions, Welsh Office, Scottish Office, | Peer bodies, WS Atkins, Audit Commission, Accounts Commission for Scotland |
| ment, Transport and Regions, Maritime and Coastguard Agency | Maritime and Coastguard Agency |
| ment, Transport and Regions | To be appointed |
| e Executive, Scottish National Health Service Executive, Welsh Office | National Health Service Executive, Scottish National Health Service Executive, Audit Commission |
| e Executive, Welsh Office, Scottish National Health Service Executive | National Health Service Executive, Scottish National Health Service Executive, Audit Commission |
| Office | HM Inspectorate of Fire Service, Scottish Office |
| Office, British Railways Board (for British Transport Police) | Her Majesty's Inspector of Constabulary, HM Inspector of Constabulary Scotland |
| Office, British Railways Board (for British Transport Police) | Her Majesty's Inspector of Constabulary, HM Inspector of Constabulary Scotland |
| Office, British Railways Board (for British Transport Police) | Her Majesty's Inspector of Constabulary, HM Inspector of Constabulary Scotland |
| Office, British Railways Board (for British Transport Police) | Her Majesty's Inspector of Constabulary, HM Inspector of Constabulary Scotland |
| orporation Board of Governors, Radio Authority | KPMG & another to be appointed |
| Welsh Office, Scottish Office | Audit Commission, Accounts Commission for Scotland |
| Welsh Office, Scottish Office | Audit Commission, Accounts Commission for Scotland |
| Welsh Office, Scottish Office | Audit Commission, Accounts Commission for Scotland |
| Welsh Office, Scottish Office | Audit Commission, Accounts Commission for Scotland |
| Welsh Office, Scottish Office | Audit Commission, Accounts Commission for Scotland |
| Welsh Office, Scottish Office | Audit Commission, Accounts Commission for Scotland |
| Welsh Office, Scottish Office | Audit Commission, Accounts Commission for Scotland |
| Welsh Office, Scottish Office | Audit Commission, National Health Service Executive, Accounts Commission for Scotland |
| Welsh Office, Scottish Office | Audit Commission, Accounts Commission for Scotland |
| ment, Transport and Regions, Maritime and Coastguard Agency | To be appointed |
| fice | National Audit Office |
| nd Industry (Posts) | To be appointed |
| nd Industry (Posts) | To be appointed |
| Security | To be appointed |
| nd Industry (Posts) | To be appointed |
| Fisheries and Food, ?(Wales), SOAEFD? | To be appointed |
| Office | DBi Associates (England and Wales) |
| artment, Scottish Office | To be appointed |
| Office | Probation Inspectorate (England and Wales) |
| | External Consultants plus peer review |
| ment, Transport and Regions | To be appointed |
| nd Industry | To be appointed |

| Sector | Name | Responsible Body |
| --- | --- | --- |
| Electricity | Provide Electricity | Office of Electricity Re |
| Gas | Provide Gas | Office of Gas Supply |
| Fuel Supplies | Supply Transport Fuel | Department of Trade a |
| | Supply Coal | Department of Trade |
| | Supply Nuclear Fuel | Nuclear Installations I |
| | Provide Oil | Department of Trade a |
| Telecommunications | Provide Telecommunications | Office of Telecommun |
| Water and Sewage | Treat Dirty Water | Office of Water Servic |
| | Supply Clean Water | Office of Water Servic |
| Financial Services | Transmit Monies | Financial Services Au |
| | Trading Markets | Financial Services Au |
| | Provide Insurance | Financial Services Au |
| | Invest and Borrow Money | Financial Services Au |
| Essential Food and Groceries | Supply Goods | Essential Foods and ( |
| | Produce Food | Essential Foods and ( |
| | Process Food | Essential Foods and ( |
| | Distribute Food | Essential Foods and ( |
| | Sell to Customer | Essential Foods and ( |
| Rail Transport | Transport People and Goods by Rail | Office of the Rail Reg |
| | Provide Rail Infrastructure | Office of the Rail Reg |
| | Transport People by Underground | Government Office fo |
| | Provide Cross-channel Rail Services | Intergovernmental Co |
| | Maintain Channel Rail Infrastructure | Intergovernmental Co |
| Air Transport | Transport People by Air | Civil Aviation Authority |
| | Provide Air Infrastructure | Civil Aviation Authority |
| Road Transport, Local Government | Provide Road Infrastructure | Department of Enviror |
| | | Government Offices |
| Sea Transport | Transport People and Goods by Sea | Department of Enviror |
| | Provide Sea Infrastructure | Department of Enviror |
| Hospitals and Healthcare | Provide Healthcare Services | National Health Servic |
| | Provide Emergency Ambulance Service | National Health Servic |
| Fire Services | Provide Fire and Rescue Service | Home Office, Scottish |
| Police | Police Emergencies | Home Office, Scottish |
| | Deal with Offences and Incidents | Home Office, Scottish |
| | Maintain Public Order | Home Office, Scottish |
| | Provide Policing Services | Home Office, Scottish |
| Broadcasting | Broadcast Information (BBC and radio only) | British Broadcasting ( |
| Local Government | Co-ordinate Emergency Response | Government Offices, |
| | Provide Housing | Government Offices, |
| | Educate People | Government Offices, |
| | Manage Sanitation and Waste Disposal | Government Offices, |
| | Register Births, Deaths and Marriages | Government Offices, |
| | Manage Death | Government Offices, |
| | Maintain Public Health | Government Offices, |
| | Provide Community and Nursing Care | Government Offices, |
| | Provide Social Services | Government Offices, |
| Sea Rescue | Provide Sea Rescue Service | Department of Enviror |
| Weather Forecasting | Provide Weather Information | The Meteorological O |
| Post and Parcels | Distribute Letters | Department of Trade |
| | Distribute Parcels | Department of Trade |
| Welfare Payments | Pay Welfare | Department of Social |
| | Operate Post Office Counters | Department of Trade |
| Flood Defence | Maintain Flood Defence | Ministry of Agriculture |
| Criminal Justice | Secure Prisoners | Home Office, Scottish |
| | Run Court System | Lord Chancellor's Dep |
| | Provide Post-sentence Support and Supervision | Home Office, Scottish |
| Tax Collection | Collect Revenue | To be appointed |
| Bus Transport | Transport People by Bus | Department of Enviror |
| Newspapers | Supply Newspapers | Department of Trade |

# Appendix 3: Departments and Agencies making returns

| Department | Agency(ies) |
| --- | --- |
| Attorney General's Office (no return from centre) | *Crown Prosecution Service* <br> *Serious Fraud Office* <br> *Treasury Solicitor's Department* |
| Cabinet Office | *Buying Agency* <br> *Central Computer and Telecommunications Agency* <br> *Central Office of Information* <br> *Civil Service College* <br> *Government Car and Dispatch Agency* <br> *Property Advisers to the Civil Estate* |
| Department of Culture Media and Sport | |
| Department for Education and Employment | *Employment Service Agency* |
| Department for International Development | |
| Department for Environment, Transport and the Regions | *Driving and Vehicle Licensing Agency* <br> *Driving Standards Agency* <br> *Highways Agency* <br> *Maritime and Coastguard Agency* <br> *Planning Inspecorate* <br> *Queen Elizabeth II Conference Centre* <br> *Vehicle Certification Agency* <br> *Vehicle Inspectorate* |
| Department of Health (including Medical Devices Agency) | *Medicines Control Agency* <br> *NHS Estates* <br> *NHS Pensions Agency* |
| Department of Social Security | |
| Department of Trade and Industry | *Companies House* <br> *Employment Tribunals* <br> *Insolvency Service* <br> *National Weights and Measures Laboratory* <br> *Patent Office* <br> *Radiocommunications Agency* |
| Export Credits and Guarantees Department | |
| Foreign and Commonwealth Office | |
| Forestry Commission | |
| Government Offices for the Regions | |
| HM Customs and Excise | |

| Department | Agency(ies) |
| --- | --- |
| HM Land Registry | |
| HM Treasury | *Debt Management Office* |
| Home Office | *Fire Service College*<br>*Forensic Science Service*<br>*Prison Service*<br>*UK Passport Agency* |
| Inland Revenue | *Valuation Office* |
| Intervention Board | |
| Lord Advocate's Department (no return from centre) | *Crown Office for Scotland* |
| Lord Chancellor's Department | |
| Ministry of Agriculture Fisheries and Food | |
| Ministry of Defence | *Army*<br>*Defence Evaluation and Research Agency*<br>*Meteorological Office*<br>*Procurement Executive*<br>*Royal Air Force*<br>*Royal Navy*<br>*United Kingdom Hydrographic Office* |
| National Savings | |
| Office for National Statistics | |
| Ordnance Survey | |
| Privy Council Office | |
| Public Record Office | |
| Royal Mint | |
| Scottish Office | *Fisheries Research Services*<br>*General Register Office for Scotland*<br>*Historic Scotland*<br>*National Archives of Scotland*<br>*Registers of Scotland*<br>*Scottish Agricultural Science Agency*<br>*Scottish Court Service*<br>*Scottish Fisheries Protection Agency*<br>*Scottish Prison Service*<br>*Student Awards Agency*<br>*Scottish Pensions Agency* |
| Welsh Office | |

# Reports by the Comptroller and Auditor General, Session 1998-99

The Comptroller and Auditor General has to date, in Session 1998-99, presented to the House of Commons the following reports under Section 9 of the National Audit Act, 1983:

Printed in the UK for The Stationery Office Limited on behalf of the
Controller of Her Majesty's Stationery Office
Dd 5068850   5/99   61743   Job No 82450